WEATHERING
THE CORPORATE
STORM

Creating Tangible Changes in the Workplace
Through Trickle-Out Collaboration

THAD CUMMINGS

WEATHERING THE CORPORATE STORM:
Creating Tangible Changes in the Workplace Through
Trickle-Out Collaboration
Copyright © 2018 Thad Cummings
All rights reserved.

ISBN: 978-0-9993850-2-9 (Paperback)
ISBN: 978-0-9993850-3-6 (E-book)

Library of Congress Control Number: 2018900278

Cover Photo Credit: Todd Reed
To purchase a copy of the photo, visit
www.ToddandBradReed.com

Printed in the United States of America

Table of Contents

An Important Note

Time is valuable in the business world. This is not intended to be an in-depth dialogue, but short, sweet and straight to the point. Too many discussions, elaborations and examples would decrease the likelihood of you reading it all. It is also intended to be a bit broad and vague in order to not pin down one industry specifically. There is so much more to this journey than a book of any size can offer so this is merely a starting place, a conversation if you will. I have added some reflecting questions at the end of each chapter to encourage you to continue the dialogue. Without actions, change does not occur and we would both be wasting our time.

I offer additional help and information on all of the topics. This book is a continuation of my first book, *Running From Fear*, which I believe is an important starting place for personal development. But if you are looking for more help with your business from building plans to create tangible change, consulting, hosting a speaking engagement or a seminar with employees and/or business leaders, please feel free to contact me at: **info@ThadCummings.com**

Best of luck to you on this journey.

Introduction

Have you ever taken a chance when you had nothing to lose?

It is that heart pounding fear and exhilaration when you step in way over your head and you are ready to give it your all. I started my first business at 18 years old working on wind energy. I looked like I was 12, but people assumed I was at least 30 because no one expects an 18-year-old to start a business. Before I knew it, I was discussing a $50-million-dollar project with a lease option of 10,000 acres in South Dakota. It came with negotiations of an interconnection agreement and a purchasing contract with the Western Area Power Administration (they control the electric grid in 15 states). Forget calling, I drove 22 hours to bring truffles to a director at a local electric company whom I would have to partner with to pull off the deal. I had no clue what I was doing and was literally flying by the seat of my pants.

I didn't realize the magnitude of the project when I was applying for financing to purchase wind turbines from General Electric. I also didn't know what I was doing when the electric company moved my wind farm project proposal just down the road (literally) and cut me out of the picture entirely. In my own perfect business world, I had always assumed that if you were good to people they would be good back. Now did I realistically have a chance at pulling that project off without major investors backing me while simultaneously being so young and inexperienced? Probably not. But I was too determined, or naïve, to see that at the time.

When the wind project was yanked out from under me, I was left twiddling my thumbs. The economy was crashing yet somehow I was still determined to "save the world." I took every odd job I could over the next year to keep paying the business's bills; I was going to school full time, and I was still chipping away at new ways to make sustainability work, albeit on a much smaller scale this time. I stumbled upon a restaurant looking to become a bit more "green," but they didn't need any wind turbines. Instead, they asked me if I could find eco-friendly products to replace their Styrofoam take-out containers. Eco-friendly products weren't common yet so I started doing research and making calls. The company I finally made contact with said they didn't have a distributor in Michigan and asked if I would be interested. What 19-year-old wouldn't be?

When my father passed away my senior year of high school, he left me with $15,000. I paid off my car and took the remaining $10,000 and bought six pallets of compostable products (cases of cutlery, cups and to-go ware made out of plants instead of petroleum). I hadn't the slightest clue on how to sell or distribute products. Heck, I didn't even know what profit margin meant as I had never even taken a business class. But the best part was I had neither pride nor an ego and nothing to lose beyond the $10,000. That meant I was willing to ask for help, ask embarrassing questions, and I was eager to learn whatever I could. I struggled relentlessly to pick up whatever accounts I could over the next two years and nearly gave up on multiple occasions. But I didn't and somehow, I prevailed.

By time I was 21 and had graduated with a degree in Natural Resource Management, I was selling $500,000 of product, had a re-distributor and another million dollars of product negotiations in the works. I owned my own compost-hauling routes, started social programs with the companies and I was eager to start additional businesses. Over time, I would grow to own stakes in several companies and even start my own non-profit. I was determined to do business differently and still save the world in the process. Now don't worry, there is a good "I lost it all" story coming, otherwise I wouldn't have the time to write this book, but more on that later.

The bigger I grew, the more I encountered people trying to take advantage of me for their own personal gain. People I was helping, people I had built companies for, people I had made tens of thousands of dollars for, people who owed me tens of thousands of dollars. Everyone was in it for themselves.

I've sat with CEOs worth $100 million to $1 million to those going bankrupt and those just starting out. I've had dozens of employees and I've worked with people who have thousands of employees. I've consulted for just about every industry from mom-and-pop shops to some of the largest corporations like: Ford, Amway, General Motors, Big 10 universities, hospital groups, restaurant groups, hotel/hospitality groups and distribution industries. I even did sustainability work with groups like McDonalds and I'm a hippie for crying out loud!

The common themes? There was not one industry that I worked with that didn't hold true to some basic consistencies; not all, but most people were in it for themselves, they weren't afraid to burn some bridges and most people had a significant amount of employees or bosses with resentment toward their jobs. The majority of people today don't last 30+ years at the same company. The ones that do don't always tend to be overly happy but feel stuck, have families dependent on their income, or are too afraid to take a chance elsewhere for fear of failure. Stress, anxiety, burnout and fatigue are everywhere. It begs to answer some hard questions:

- Why do employees, managers, and even CEOs count the minutes until Friday and pray that Monday is a lifetime away?

- Why are people always looking for another job even if they aren't willing to take a chance and leave their current one?

- Why are people so miserable in the workplace, so stressed out, or constantly complaining about co-workers or their boss?

I've worked for companies, I've owned companies, I've consulted for companies. I've been the employee, the manager, the boss, and the outsider looking in. What I want to share with you today are the largest roadblocks that keep companies from being holistically healthy. There is no such thing as a perfect company or job, that isn't the point. But whether your goal is better relations with your co-workers, higher customer satisfaction, higher employee satisfaction, less stress, anger or drama, better leaders, better sales, better growth, or even just more profit, I can promise you that your job or company cannot and will not thrive long term without some new principles and directions.

Let's get to work.

PART 1

SIT

Be still, listen and understand

"Never miss a good chance to shut up"
–Will Rogers

1

WHY SHOULD YOU CARE?
It isn't a trick question.

Now most people I've worked with don't dislike their job entirely; there is no such thing as a perfect job, even if you did get your dream job. But we live in a world where almost everyone really does count the minutes until Friday and is praying Monday is a lifetime away. Why are we so desperate to get away from something we will spend at least 1/3 of our adult life doing? We live on the notions of extended weekends and one-week vacations. Heck, it is even negotiated into hiring contracts on every level. One of the first questions a boss has to address or a new employee secretly wants to ask is, "How much time am I going to get away from this thing you are really trying to get me to do in the first place?"

I sometimes chuckle at the notion because if you know anything about running companies, there is no such thing as a vacation, holiday, or extended weekends. I went almost 8 years without taking a real vacation; I was miserable. In today's world of connection, everyone has your cell phone number, there is always a fire to put out, someone is always unhappy, and when someone makes a mistake, well let's just say I've had calls that the world was going to end if I didn't deliver a case of 12oz coffee cups on a Saturday morning.

Employees now often feel the same burdens their bosses carry as technology advances and the demand for connection along with it. There is pressure to work extra hours, do emails on the weekends, and even carry your phone with you on vacation. There is nothing worse than a mother or a father trying to push their kid on a swing at the park and walking away to answer the ceaseless ringing of a cellphone or typing one handed emails as the kiddo yells "higher!"

If the bosses and management don't directly demand it, our customers will. We are hell-bent on customer service and pleasing everyone because nowadays someone can publicly attack you if you slip up in the slightest. If your rating on Google is not at least 4/5 stars, well your image is toast. So we become chained to the customer, to efficiencies, to our images, and to making a profit. We become chained to pleasing our bosses, to keeping employees happy, to performance and to bigger paychecks.

Who ultimately loses? You do.

I don't care if you are an employee or a manager or a boss or a CEO. For example, a CEO may crack down on the managers and the managers pass it on to the employees. The employees will become disgruntled and fight back, or get passive, or get frustrated and bring the mood down which will affect the work of the managers and the stress will eventually make its way back to the CEO. There is a constant cycle of never-ending teeter-totters trying to please everyone.

The employee suffers, the management suffers and in many cases, even the customers suffer.

In part or in whole, everyone suffers.

Companies systematically function better, make more money, have higher social and environmental impacts, and have healthier and happier employees when all employee fears are addressed head on at all levels. Leaders become more effective, employees have more work ethic, and customers are more satisfied. I don't care what your motivation is for reading this book because I don't believe in trickle-down economics.

I believe in trickle-out collaboration.

Let me break it down. If employees and bosses are happier, work life is less stressful. If work life is less stressful, customers are going to be happier. If customers are happier, the company will be more successful. If the company is more successful, the pressure and weight of all members of the business will take home less anger and frustrations into their personal life. When you bring more joy into your home and less work-related stress, there is a statistically higher likelihood that you will be better engaged with your friends, your partners, your families, even your children, if you have them. If you treat the people in your life better, then there is a chance that they may treat other people better. Before you know it, we are solving the world's problems because everyone is harmoniously working together serving the ingenuity of the greater good.

Boom.

Now that the world's problems are solved because you choose to give your coworker the benefit of the doubt and not yell at them, let's end the book there.

Funny, sure. But seriously, there is truth in small deeds; there is truth in trickle-out collaboration. There is no such thing as a perfect company. No customer, employee, or boss will ever be completely satisfied. It isn't human nature, even though that sounds like a pitiful excuse if you ask me. But let's also be honest and say that we could all use less stress in our lives.

When stress comes in we tend to immediately project it outwards. It is much easier to get mad at our bosses and co-workers than it is to take responsibility. I'm not saying your co-workers, your boss or your employees don't make some extremely frustrating decisions that can cost you time, head-aches, and resources. What I am saying is that the more you are frustrated with someone else, the more you are ultimately giving them power over your joy. If you take one thing away from this book, know that the power for you to live a life full of abundance is not dependent upon the actions of others, as difficult as that can be at times. That person who seems to be making your life more difficult is also facing struggles of his or her own. This conversation starts with tangible ways to regain control of you, because a healthier and happier you only makes the rest of us stronger.

I don't care what level of the company you are on or if your company consists of 1 person or 1,000, there are con-crete steps you can take to improve the overall health and sustainability of your workplace. It doesn't start with point-ing the finger at someone else, it starts with you. You are only responsible for your own physiological and psychologi-cal wellbeing; don't place all the weight on Jamie in Human Resources to save the day. Let's get to work, let's ask some hard questions and reflect on ways we can all work towards improving the quality of work life.

Do you want more joy and less stress from your job? Let's get started at the basics with fear because, well, it's everywhere and in everything.

Ps: bring some snacks in for your co-workers... everyone loves food and a little effort to show that you care and are trying goes a long way. Bonus points for homemade (assuming you do it yourself).

CHAPTER 1 NOTES AND REFLECTIONS

How would you rate your overall satisfaction with your job? What factors contribute to this? Take away from it? What do you think your co-workers would say their satisfaction is? Have you ever asked them?

_____

_____

_____

_____

_____

_____

_____

_____

_____

_____

_____

_____

_____

_____

_____

2

FEAR, FEAR EVERYWHERE,
with no sign of relief

Many people who became successful in the business world are all given a similar label – "fearless." How many times have you heard speeches or toasts or award ceremonies where someone gives all of the credit to the "fearless leader" that brought the team to success? Overcoming fears in business means having the tenacity to do what needs to get done. It involves a lot of determination and most of all, it requires a lot of sacrifice. No one builds a company, gets promoted or becomes successful overnight. It can take months to years to decades for many to reach their full potential, if there even is such a thing. But what happens in the process of the pursuit of success often means other values and other people are pushed to the side.

I remember my first taste of large success when I landed my first hotel group. I was going to supply all of their disposable products with the industry's highest level of sustainable and compostable products. At the time, I was a senior in college struggling to grow my distribution company with no purchasing power and a meager $22,000 in gross annual

21

sales. Even if I had 100% margin, I wouldn't be able to survive off of that after paying the bills. So I asked if I could put my degree to use and focus my senior capstone project on doing a full zero-waste analysis on a local hotel group. This would entail the suitability of the products, training the employees, feasibility studies, a cost analysis, marketing, you name it. My professor agreed and I got to work hand in hand with the purchasing managers at the hotel collecting data and understanding their analytics. I built a comprehensive cost analysis, looked at logistics, competitive overviews, made a business plan, and even entered into a business plan competition with my work where I took second place.

What really changed was not just all of the information I learned on doing a deep dive of my own industry but how I approached my sales pitch. You see, I didn't have purchasing power and couldn't get new accounts because my prices were too high. But if I landed an account this size, I would actually move up two brackets and my purchasing power would allow me to be significantly cheaper than my largest competitors. So I bid the project based on winning, not where I was currently at.

It was working and I was terrified. It wasn't the minor leagues anymore and I was now taking accounts from national companies, companies with high levels of service, power and financial influence. What if I couldn't deliver, or perform, or handle the inventory or cash flow needed to get to this done? For crying out loud, I was manually typing every invoice into a Word document; I didn't even have accounting software to keep track of inventory or accounts receivable. My accounting department was my memory. But I pushed my fears aside and jumped in.

The hotel group interviewed my suppliers to make sure I could handle a company this size. They were a large company with major contracts and were about to take a gamble on a kid no one had ever heard of. You don't take risks like that in business to save a few bucks when you know the headaches it will cause. But they saw my passion for it and what I could bring to the table. Overnight, my company grew sevenfold and I now had the power to compete with the big companies. The companies that sold, not thousands, but millions in food service products per year.

I had nearly shut the company down twice in that previous year since I couldn't make enough as a waiter to pay for my bills and I was growing weary of endless work with little results. After my big break, I was installing a trailer hitch onto my two-door, bright yellow, embarrassingly ugly Ford Focus as I waited in line with the semi trucks for a loading dock to make my deliveries. Some times it would take me all day running back and forth from my warehouse to downtown Grand Rapids. It would take my tiny car and trailer 4-6 trips, what a normal supplier could do in 15 minutes. But they worked with me until I could afford to buy a bigger car, then a minivan, then a cargo van and I grew to accommodate the world I was now living in.

Why? Because a guy named Bill coached me into starting a company and a guy named Russ let me use the corner of his warehouse for free. And a lady named Griff let me go completely off the charts and do a capstone project that had never been approved before. A guy named Bruce took a chance on signing a purchase order with a kid and a lady named Peg made me fierce in standing my on own in front of crowds. Over eight years, dozens of friends and strangers chipped in to help me, to guide me, to coach me, to clean up my accounting, to show me spreadsheets, to teach me tactics and skills and traits in all matters of business.

But the more I grew, the less there was a fear of failure. I was becoming more confident in my success. But as the success evolved, so did the fears; now there was a fear of losing it all. I suddenly had dozens of accounts, hundreds of thousands in sales, payroll, cash flow issues, inventory issues, product failure issues, employee issues, and every issue in between. I remember the first threat of lawsuit when one of my coffee cups leaked coffee onto a customer. When someone microwaved a soup container that caught fire. When I couldn't afford to run payroll and buy inventory at the same time because so many accounts were back due in paying me.

The phone never stopped going off and there was always a fire to put out. When people asked me what I did for a living I would always jokingly say, "I'm a firefighter, all I do is put out fires." Something was always going wrong and it was ultimately up to me to fix it. Sleep became dismal and the more I became consumed in my own fears and stresses, the less concerned I became about the wellbeing of my friends and family and employees. The more my personal life suffered, the more my work life suffered, the more my employees suffered. Then my health began to give way and my fears took on a whole new meaning.

My back was in such spasms I could barely put my shoes on some days but I would slowly manage to load thousands of pounds of boxes and make the deliveries when there was no choice. I remember when infections ravaged my body and my immune system began to decline so bad that I was constantly sick. There is no feeling like unloading a semi truck of pallets in 90-degree weather when you have a fever. I even reached my lowest point when my heart went into a trance and I had a panic attack in the middle of a delivery and found myself lying on the floor of a loading dock in a smear of truck grease as an employee called an ambulance.

What was the gift in all of these difficult scenarios? I was able to understand fear from all angles, not because I read about it or went to a lecture on it, but because I personally tasted it. The fear of being an employee living paycheck to paycheck. The fear of starting something new, the fear of failure, the fear of the unknowns and the what-ifs. The fears of success, of growing too slowly, growing too quickly. The fear of losing it all. The fear of not being able to pay credit card bills or employees. The fear of firing people, the fear of taking a chance on someone new. Fears with my physical health and even the fear of asking for help.

I haven't met a single employee, manager, boss or consultant who isn't battling some kind of fear in the workforce. Fear stems from two trains of thought; fear of not having control and fear of not being enough. These two notions can be found at the root sources of all of the fears, struggles and insecurities we face. Have a resistance to the word fear? Replace it with the word stress, anger, frustration or maybe be bold and admit you have some anxieties. Because what does it all boil down to in the end? Fear that you can't pay your bills? Fear your boss may fire you? Fear that thing won't get done right if you don't do it yourself? Fear you will lose that account? Fear you won't make it or fear of not being the biggest and most powerful?

The what-if questions in our attempts to control the outcomes and expectations of our lives lead to a toxic demise enshrouded in unnecessary despair that can consume us, even with the best of intentions. I'm not attempting to proclaim that if you follow a ten-step process, all of the storms in life will disappear. Instead, this conversation is about re-engaging those storms from a different perspective. When we challenge that perspective, we ask new questions that put our joy and relationships as the focal point, not our bank accounts. This is what gives us the power to live a life full of more abundance and joy. That is worth sharing with our workplace because we all know there is no shortage of stress.

Step 1 of trickle-out collaboration: admit your fears. In order to face your fears and insecurities, you have to first admit that you have them. Big or small, many or few, seemingly powerful or meager, write them down. Don't let your ego get in the way; I promise you that we all have fears, otherwise the world would be perfect and there would be no need for this discussion.

CHAPTER 2 NOTES AND REFLECTIONS

Identify some of your fears. What are some of your co-worker's fears? What about the fears of your bosses and managers? What fears are holding you back? What fears are holding your workplace back? Does your company have a safe way to discuss these? Are you able to go to your boss? Are you able to go to your employees?

_____

_____

_____

_____

_____

_____

_____

_____

_____

_____

_____

_____

_____

_____

_____

3

KILLING COMPANIES,
when fear holds precedent

Historically, kings, empires and even religions have used certain precedents from their decrees or texts to create, as well as justify, heinous crimes. It's a notion of power, a notion of being right, and the notion that, if used with force, the message will be instilled. Now has this ever sustained itself? I think over the last several thousand years of great empires and ruling kingdoms, there is always one commonality; they eventually crumble. Fear cannot retain power long term. How fear is used to control continuously evolves, but the "why" behind it doesn't:

If you're not growing, you're dying.

You think the empires, kings and religions of old were barbaric in their ruthless quest for power? The modern day precedent of using fear to control the work place is the same thought-process that has been around for thousands of years. I have never met a single organization, business, corporation, even non-profit that isn't always grasping for more. More sales, more income, more profit, more products, more equity, more space, more, more, more. It consumes us and the message becomes simple – if you are not growing by x% each year, something is terribly wrong. Joe needs to get fired, Sara needs a demotion, we need a new sales strategy or we need to re-outfit our company. We are as barbaric as our ancestors, just with less physical violence. Let's nickname this thought process our "barbaric mentality."

Honestly, I'm no different. I carried around a dusty bottle of champagne for 6 years. I bought it when I purchased my first house and was going to have friends over to celebrate. But life got busy. So it was when I landed my first big client. Then when I hit $500,000 in sales. When I hired my first employees. Heck, it even became the same bottle that was going to be popped when I sold my first company. But that same bottle collected more and more dust and remained closed. There was never a true celebration because there was always more to do and always more to accomplish.

We may poke fun at the simple things in life. The desire for a bigger flat screen television, a larger home, smarter phone or nicer car, but this mentality of "more" comes into our work life. It is not wrong to desire a promotion, higher pay, or more sales. However, when those desires become the focal point, we develop an insatiable appetite in the endless pursuit of bigger, better and more.

This mentality inevitably projects the message that nothing is ever good enough. The single largest complaint I have ever heard from any employee is, "I don't feel like my work is valued – my boss thinks I'm not good enough." What if that was your friend, your spouse, or your child uttering those words to you? Yet we have all felt that feeling in the workplace. When you finally stop trying harder and harder and hit that feeling of despair. That feeling you weren't good enough. You couldn't finish the project in time, you didn't make the quota, you didn't land the account, there were no holiday bonuses. Whatever it was, something was not good enough; even if you were growing, it wasn't by enough. Did that inspire you or make you feel like you could accomplish more? Of course not. Yet this is much of the culture we have in our jobs today.

Yes, most of us try harder for a while, but we all have a breaking point. The result of our barbaric mentality is stress, fatigue, anxiety and despair. Worst-case scenario, people feel chained to their job and find other ways to cope like booze, Netflix, sports or medications. Especially when the work lacks any form of fulfillment. Even scarier are the people I meet who are stuck paying mortgages or tuitions or medical bills or debts and have no choice but to endure it in order to take care of themselves or their loved ones.

This is not a conversation to shame and guilt our co-workers, employees or bosses. Countering a negative emotion with another negative emotion never resolves any issues. We aren't perfect and our success is not actually defined by just our numbers. It's a hard pill to swallow for both employers and employees, but it's one we need to swallow if we long for the businesses we work for and with to survive long-term without an endless turnover rate. It's a pill we need to swallow so that we can set our pride and egos aside and have challenging, yet real, dialogue with all aspects of the company. The barbaric mentality can ruin all prospects of trickle-out collaboration.

I've seen entire businesses collapse, mergers dissolve, and acquisitions fail because pride and egos got in the way. When communication was set aside for the need to be right, greed or because it was "someone else's fault," it comes at the cost of friendships, jobs and often times our sanity. These are the games we play to climb the corporate ladder, get a foothold above a co-worker, prove someone wrong or to strong-arm the competition.

If it isn't your fault, then make it your responsibility; at least then you have some control and stake in the game to change the circumstance. You can help resolve and be a part of the solution. If you are an employee looking at your boss, have you sat down with them in an appropriate manner and explain to them without attacking to give them the opportunity to become a better boss? If you are a boss, did you make it safe for your employees to come and speak to you and voice concerns? Did either side communicate in an effective way so that everyone's voice was heard and understood, not demanded?

If you are a boss, you know how many mistakes your employees make. But if you are an employee, you know how many mistakes your boss makes. Part of the reality in this situation is asking what you had control of in the situation. Attempt to decipher what role you had to play in it, directly or indirectly. Stop pointing the finger at everyone else's mistakes and own your own mistakes. Blame belongs in high school gossip circles, not a business. It is toxic and makes everyone bitter and resentful. Take time to set the precedent in a public way that you aren't perfect but you are going to try to be better. Be bold and ask for feedback on how you can do so. When you get that feedback, don't get defensive or attack back, but sit with it and get curious about it

We can spend up to one third of our adult waking hours at work. The people we work with can have significant insights and revelations that we should be listening to. Your character is not defined by the size of your paycheck or the growth of the company, it is defined by the wealth of your relationships. Cheesy, yes, but also very true. It is time to redefine the definition of "growth."

Companies should not be defined by growing numbers but by the interconnectedness and stability of the teamwork as well as the health of the employees. You cannot get to work without depending on someone who made your car, who paved the roads, who harvested that coffee bean half way around the world or made your clothes. That email didn't send and your phone didn't ring because you wished for it to be so.

Humble yourself. It is good for you, I promise.

You are interconnected into the very fabric of this entire community. We are all dependent upon one another in the very essence of our existence. It is time we treated our coworkers the same. Your business does not survive without Jake answering the phones at the front desk, Sarah handling accounting or Jessica having the tenacity to start a company in the first place. Acknowledge the interconnectedness that you have a job in collaboration with the work of multitudes of people and businesses.

It will take some of the weight off of your shoulders to revel in the smallness of who you are while simultaneously opening you up for the opportunity to see those around you. If you decide to keep all of the weight, you burn out, and we all lose.

Step 2 of trickle-out collaboration: redefine enough.
Take time to realize the perilous effects the barbaric mentality of "if you are not growing, you're dying" has on our culture. In the simplest notion, it will eventually disrupt all aspects of our relationships when our pride and egos set precedence and communication is all but lost. That is how fear wins the day and the company dies, even if it is perceived to be growing. You are one of seven billion people; you will never be the richest, strongest, or most powerful. So what is it that you are really longing for in your pursuit to define "enough"? Let's honor our humility and open up new doors of communication to value the interconnectedness of our community as a whole when we realize the empires of old are gone and we cannot conquer it all.

CHAPTER 3 NOTES AND REFLECTIONS

How do you define success at your job? How do you define "enough"? What are the overarching goals of the company you run or work for? Do you feel isolated or independent in your work? Do you value the interconnectedness of your community?

_____

_____

_____

_____

_____

_____

_____

_____

_____

_____

_____

_____

_____

_____

_____

_____

4

BURNING OUT AND WALKING AWAY,

when the candle goes out

Everyone loves talking about sustainability these days yet nobody talks about the sustainability of the employees or employers, their mental health and their wellbeing. We especially don't talk about the health of our personal lives. We don't discuss how the impact of overworking a person can ruin the dynamics of families or friends which can further ruin the welfare of the individual which can ultimately come back to ruin a company because companies are made out of people. There is another false narrative we share in the workplace:

Working overtime is strength, taking a day off is weakness.

When I ran my companies, there wasn't a single day that went by I wasn't working on something, or checking emails, or answering calls and texts. I remember the first week I ever worked over 100 hours. That meant I had to work at least 14 hours a day for 7 straight days. If I were being honest, I was actually a bit arrogant and smugly proud of my work ethic when I compared it to those around me. One company wasn't enough, I needed two. Two wasn't enough, could I start three? $100,000 in sales wasn't enough, I needed a million. A million isn't going to allow me to make enough extra money to sustain my non-profit, I need to set my sights bigger.

I worked tirelessly and the response from everyone around me was eager enthusiasm. I was applauded for my drive by everyone, except those closest to me. The ones who saw what it was doing to me, my relationships and my health. I was plagued with stress and anxiety that a Xanax couldn't touch. My social life didn't exist if it wasn't connected to work. Even when I was physically present to my partner and child, I was a million miles away. Ever come home from a long day and your partner just wants to have a conversation yet you are checking your phone during dinner or looking at the television? I was anything but present in my home life, as difficult as it is to admit and own.

I hit my peak sickness, my health collapsed, my family left and ultimately, my businesses crumbled. Our culture applauds work ethic, going the extra mile, "blood, sweat and tears" to make it, whatever "it" is. The result? Many of my friends were overweight, binge drinking the weekends, getting divorces, facing health issues, taking medications, doing anything they could to just get by another day. We laugh at Europe where some countries mandate a 35-hour maximum workweek. We call them lazy yet dismiss how much statistically and medically healthier and happier many of those countries are compared to the United States.

We don't discuss things like work-life balance. We don't discuss the need for time to recharge, time to settle, time to disconnect. Instead we force a demand that if you do not respond to that email, voicemail or text within 30 minutes, you have failed your company or your clients, you are indeed the lazy one and we will find someone better. The rapacious demand to be constantly connected, constantly working and constantly performing affects all aspects of our lives negatively.

Even if you don't want to engage about a co-worker's personal life or wellbeing, you should care about the reality that the company is going to suffer if the people in it are suffering. Ever walked into the office and just felt the weight of the tension spewing onto your lap? Ever been on the receiving end of a boss who just had a fight with their spouse and is now coming after you for spending an extra dollar on a stapler?

We can push ourselves, our employees and our companies to the edge over and over again. But the inevitable result, what happens when you "burn the candle from both ends"? Burn out, collapse and walking away. Similar to the barbaric mentality, fear of not being enough wins the day, not the health of the business. We must take time to further redefine the definition of what is enough and that involves believing you, as a person, are enough; that your worth is not defined by your success and you deserve to take time for you.

Taking a day off is not weakness. Caring for the wellbeing of your mental and physical self is not selfish. It is important, it is necessary, it is vital to the welfare of everyone you are interconnected to. We are only able to bring to the table the strength with which we are able to carry our own weight. The courage to care for yourself is what brings fortitude back to those you engage your life with, not burning out and walking away.

Don't be surprised if it is hard to do, especially in a culture that does everything it can to tell us we don't deserve it. I remember the first time I tried to take a day off; I lasted a few hours before picking my cell phone back up. I was bored and I didn't know what to do without some form of electronic gadget. I also felt useless to society, like I wasn't contributing anything so who was I to take a break? Don't forget, we are mainly discussing the issues of the work-life-balance. You still have errands, kids, bills, laundry and all matters of life waiting for you outside the office. When you can't handle your work life, how can you make time to be present for your friends, kids and family? When you can't make time for those around you, how are you going to find time to be present for yourself?

Step 3 of trickle out-collaboration: self-care. The most crucial piece of advice I can share is to start off small. I would tend to try and make a big to-do list of self-care that I wouldn't be able to keep up with, then I'd get frustrated, then I'd quit altogether. You don't have to move to a monastery in the middle of the mountains to find sanity again. Keep it simple and build from there. If you can't find an hour to go do yoga right now, then take 5 minutes to sit in a quiet space and just take deep breaths without distractions or technology. Set boundaries and learn to say no, you can't be everywhere and everything to everyone. And most importantly, reduce times of connection. Find periods throughout the day to turn off the computer, put the cell-phone on silent and get away from all technology. We don't become experts in anything over-night, and that includes taking care of ourselves.

Lastly, learn to laugh at yourself. Whatever you think is so incredibly important, I promise you the world will keep spinning and the sun will rise tomorrow.

CHAPTER 4 NOTES AND REFLECTIONS

Do you feel overly connected? How? In what ways might you feel overworked? Do you give yourself time to breathe and take breaks? How do you engage in self-care?

_____

_____

_____

_____

_____

_____

_____

_____

_____

_____

_____

_____

_____

_____

_____

_____

_____

_____

PART 2

THINK

Make a plan

"The less men think, the more they talk"
–Charles de Montesquieu (circa 1725)

5

WHAT RELATIONSHIP?

Like it or not, everyone is your teacher,
including yourself

I f I asked you to explain your business or what you did
for a living, I bet you could tell me it to the tee in under
three minutes. But if I asked you to tell me who you are
or what makes you come alive, most people would fumble
over their words. Now if I took it one step further and asked
you to explain to me your employee's or co-worker's lives
and what makes them tick, most would hardly be able to
give me 30 seconds.

We rarely know the joys and sorrows of those around us
beyond the surface level conversations that take place over the
coffee pot. It doesn't tend to go deeper than, "How was your
weekend?" or "Did you have a good holiday?". Now if I asked
simply why that is, the most generic responses revolve around
the notion that this is work, not a social party and there isn't
enough time for that; keep your personal life at home.

Granted, there isn't time to spend hours a day engaging
every co-worker, but I think the thing behind the thing here
goes deeper than that. We oftentimes don't know the lives,

or take the time to engage the lives of our co-workers because we don't even take the time to engage those closest to us or ourselves. In the healthiest of relationships, there is a strong feeling of connection and safety. Part of your mental welfare is dependent upon the health of the relationships around you. If you cannot safely confide your joys and sorrows in life, then the bottling of emotions will leave a feeling of isolation. And we wonder why people often report feeling so alone in their struggles.

It doesn't matter what your circumstances are, we are all facing battles of some kind. The storms of life will always be knocking on your door, some times harder than others. But to have healthy relationships with others starts with having a healthy relationship with yourself. You are your first teacher. Do you suffer from body aches, headaches, anxiety, acid reflux, or high blood pressure? Our bodies give us many warning signs that something is <u>not working.</u> Do you struggle with stress, anger, anxiety or fatigue? Do you take time to eat well, exercise, find mental or spiritual care?

We often lose sight of the warning signs within our own body until it is too late. The health issues I spoke about earlier didn't come overnight. Some took months or years to develop. It began with a very simple acid reflux issue. Then gastritis, then leaky gut, and in time, the struggles with anxiety developed when my heart began to struggle. It wasn't until the end when I became riddled with systemic infections and turned yellow with jaundice that I was in serious peril. I had countless warning signs before it got to that point. Yet the same reason I didn't realize my co-worker had been up crying all night is the same reason I didn't stop and take a breath for myself; there was never enough time and there were always more important things to be doing.

I hope you are beginning to see a pattern around the word "enough." In truth, there was nothing more important I could have been doing.

If you cannot care for the physical and psychological wellbeing of yourself, you will not have the capability to be present for those around you. The ability to be present and have empathy is a dying art in a culture based on speed and efficiency. You cannot bottle up the pain of losing a loved one in an elevator pitch, nor would you ever expect someone to. So don't treat yourself that way; it must begin with you.

How you treat others is a reflection of how you treat yourself.

When you can take time to have compassion and empathy on yourself and care for yourself, that will trickle out into the relationships at your workplace. It begins with grace. Give yourself grace on your imperfections, on your shortcomings, on the mistakes you have made and will make again. If you cannot give yourself grace, how would you ever give grace to another? These are the building blocks that move our relationships forward and ultimately our entire workplace.

Starting with grace allows for the opportunity that there may be more than meets the eye. At some point in our life, we have all said the phrase, "walk a mile in my/his/her shoes." But we hardly ever actually even consider the possibility of the world another person may be going through. Even those you know best, your closest friends, your family, your spouse, I promise you that you do not know the entirety of their life or their struggles. Our culture is instilled upon taking everything personally. It binds us to instant judgments and resentments when anyone says something slightly off from our viewpoints. Extending grace outwards means acknowledging that you may not know the whole story of another, or even yourself.

Did that person really need to scream at you in traffic for making a mistake or do they perhaps have more things going on in their life? Is Steve yelling at you or did he just get in a fight with his kid? If you don't ask, you will never see the thing behind the thing that we are all facing. If you take every action of another personally, you will never be able to see the pain, the despair, the stress and anxiety or sheer exhaustion that may be behind their eyes. If our life is going perfect, we never need to attempt to harm or ruin someone else. We hurt people when we are hurting ourselves.

I learn more and more about my own viewpoints and desires as the years progress. It's amazing how steadfast I was in certain ways that I would not even relate to today. Things I might have even attacked others for. It is important to stay in touch and ask those same hard questions of ourselves, all the time. It is a learning journey, not one and done. To be fair, forgiveness is not a "get out of jail free" card for everyone to harm another without regard. But when we enter into healthy relationships with ourselves, we must forgive ourselves for those imperfections and that will allow us the hindsight to forgive others. This is how we foster the future moving forward.

How does every revolution start? How does every movement begin? One person takes a step forward and a community comes together. Your workplace is merely a community. Companies and workplaces as a whole are strongest and make the most impact when the company is a single unit moving forward. Communities are the strength of individual units coming together. You cannot be responsible for the whole community, but you can set precedent for how the community cares for itself in building that unity.

Healthy relationships take time to foster, especially when they didn't exist before. Don't expect instant results. Things did not get hard overnight and they will not get resolved overnight. So don't let impatience, expectations, or greed win the day. We all know the story of the revolution that ends when one person decides they deserve a bit more than somebody else. A bit more power, or wealth, or entitlement and the whole thing collapses.

I'm better than you syndrome.

Nothing will destroy a company faster than one that is built upon "survival of the fittest." Leaders tend to think that a strong sense of competition will ultimately make the company grow the quickest. In some cases, this is true, but the quickest to rise also tend to be the quickest to fall, especially when an empire is not built on a stable foundation.

When we lose the ability to realize that everyone is our teacher, we become entitled and feel like we are better than them. That is when differences are no longer seen as opportunities to learn a new or challenging perspective, but become barriers. Barriers are built into walls and no one's voice is heard. Whether through fear or shame or denial or guilt, when voices are silenced, everything becomes fragile and it takes very little disturbance to shake the entire building.

To be heard is to be known, to be known is to feel vital, to feel vital is to have ownership in the direction of that in which you serve. Employees and bosses must feel like their opinion matters because it does. Even if their opinion is not the specific direction moving forward, it still matters. Differences of opinions are how we see things from contrasting lenses which allow us to evolve and progress forward in not only business, but in life. No company has ever survived by staying static and I guarantee you do not have the exact same beliefs you do now as you did when you were a child, in most cases 10 years ago, and even quite commonly, a year ago.

We depend on the elasticity of change; we depend on our ability to be dynamic. You did not develop your opinions on your own, you did not learn what you have learned on your own, you did not become an expert on your own. There is a wonderful gift in realizing that everyone is our teacher. Young, old, experienced or not, we all are bringing unique perspectives to the table. It does not make them all right, but don't discount them simply because they could be wrong.

Step 4 of trickle-out collaboration: inward reflections. How do you need to take better care of yourself? When you are no longer drowning in your own junk, you can come back to the office and be present for those around you and the issues at hand. When you can be present, the struggles of others and the company can be heard. When the issues can be heard, new ideas, growth and innovation can be fostered. The equal units of community coming together will strengthen the company as a whole.

Take the first step – healthy relationships start with you.

CHAPTER 5 NOTES AND REFLECTIONS

How do you care for yourself? Do you invest in the livelihood of your co-workers? What avenues exist within your company to allow employee feedback to foster healthy relationships? What steps can you take to improve your own wellbeing and with those around you?

_____

_____

_____

_____

_____

_____

_____

_____

_____

_____

_____

_____

_____

_____

6

HOW DO YOU DEFINE YOUR IMAGE?

what story do you tell?

When I started a business based on helping companies become zero-waste, I faced one minor obstacle. Michigan held the third lowest tipping rates for landfills in the country (the price people are charged to dispose of waste). It was cheaper for Canada to export their trash across the border to Michigan than dispose of it in their own landfills. When I say we are the nation's wastebasket, I didn't mean that metaphorically. So why not start a company to take on an industry that has every financial incentive to not go zero-waste? Turns out there are a lot of politics and lobbying and corruption even in the waste industry, who knew. But alas, if I could make it work in Michigan, I was confident I could make it work anywhere.

Slowly but surely I took on the corporate titans of my industry. Little by little I developed a demand for my services. I realized that if one company made a move to become more sustainable, that image sells, which meant their competitors must try and follow suit. We live in a world that is starting to define itself by sustainability more and more but most importantly by businesses and people that care.

When Walmart begins selling organic, you know that Walmart didn't wake up one day wondering if they should attempt to sell a product that cost significantly more. That goes against the fabric of selling the cheapest products around. Instead, grassroots education evolved into small groceries which created a demand for a company like Whole Foods or Trader Joes which evolved a demand that Walmart needed to fill in order to stay competitive. Consumer demand drives the workplace because every product we purchase as individuals casts a vote on what we want to see in our community; it determines who gets our money and our resources.

In my industry, I was a cup of water in an ocean. There's no shame in admitting it was a multi-billion dollar industry that I held a fraction of a fraction of one percent in. However, when companies wanted the best, they didn't call my competitors even though they had plenty of options with their current suppliers – they called me. They called me because I had a passion for what I was doing and I built my image around it. I didn't just sell a product, I was knowledgeable. There was hardly a single question you could ask me about my industry that I didn't know. If I didn't know it, I was going to find out and get back to you that day. And when I sold a compostable coffee cup, it didn't mean much if I didn't offer a way to compost that coffee cup. And when I offered a way to compost that coffee cup it didn't mean much if I couldn't train the employees on how to sort trash. And that didn't mean much if it didn't come with marketing and PR, which didn't work well if it wasn't intrinsically simple for anyone and everyone. And none of that meant anything if there wasn't a story to tell behind it all.

If I couldn't provide the service, I held partnerships that could. If I couldn't be the solution, I would help my customers find the solution. It wasn't about making the most money or having all the control from my competitors, it was about building a precedent for companies to do things better because that would trickle out to the employees, which would trickle into their homes and their communities. I wasn't above getting my hands dirty and I nicknamed myself a "glorified dumpster diver." I was never afraid to sort through someone's trash and do a waste audit myself.

I had an image for sustainability but I had a reputation for caring about the relationships of my clients. This meant I hardly ever placed a cold call or did a lick of advertising. To be honest, I hate sales and cold calls; there is nothing worse to me than bugging somebody to buy something. I've actually never taken a class on sales training because using conventional tactics felt more like pulling teeth. So I developed my own and almost everything was through word of mouth.

I've consulted with companies who had a terrible reputation in the community. But they were wealthy and powerful and oftentimes the only option. They controlled the marketplace so it didn't matter. Yet the first option their customers would have to switch to a competitor, they would take it in a heartbeat. It's not the kind of image you want in order to be successful long term. You cannot sacrifice your employees or co-workers for the greater good. The viability of a company to be holistic is to not only tell a story well, but to live it well, where all aspects of the enterprise hold weight in serving a great good.

Your product or service is only half of the narrative. It is no longer good enough to just have a good product, you also need to care. It is statistically proven to be one of the most important deciding factors amongst all millennials. Like it or not, millennials are the next generation to dominate the marketplace. The demand to care about more than just profit and sales is one of the greatest revolutions to shake up the marketplace.

Questions today are not just about quality of the product or service, but where do you source, how do you pay your suppliers and employees, what is your environmental footprint and what are your social impacts in the community? We are all telling a story. How are you different? Don't wait until you are out of business to care.

Step 5 of trickle-out collaboration: define your image. Don't walk into the lobby and read some placard that sounds nice. Start a survey, hold a meeting, ask your fellow co-workers what is actually important to them, to the clients and to the community. Redefine your image collectively, not just what the marketing department thought would appease the millennials.

CHAPTER 6 NOTES AND REFLECTIONS

What is your story behind it? What are you doing with your wealth and power to make a difference in your community? What are you doing to make a difference in the world? And if I come to your business, are your co-workers going to say that they feel a part of that mission?

_____

_____

_____

_____

_____

_____

_____

_____

_____

_____

_____

_____

_____

_____

7

BUILD A COMPANY WORTH WORKING FOR,

bring the opposites together

I love listening to a philosopher like Alan Watts when he instructs us to follow our passions and pursue joy in life, not wealth. It's wonderful, but the truth is most people aren't going to do that. For better or worse, we are going to continue living in a consumerist-based culture for the foreseeable future. So we don't all get to do our dream jobs, but it doesn't mean this job has to suck.

Most children don't say "I can't wait to grow up and work in an office some day." No, as kids, we long for adventure, for inspiration, we long to serve and help others. Yet it is all too common that most people I have engaged with tell me their work feels meaningless, like they serve no purpose or aren't adding to the greater good. I don't care if you are an accountant or a janitor or you make sandwiches or you run companies, you provide a service that is needed in our community.

If someone wasn't a cashier at my grocery store or farming vegetables, it would be really difficult for me to buy food to sustain my life. A good friend of mine was once the lead pastor at a mega-church. He shared a story when someone came up and asked him, "How does it feel to be famous in the Christian world?" A year later he was helping me mop floors at my restaurant. He climbed the corporate ladder (so to speak) in the Christian world and was at the very top. Now, he would have been perceived as being at the bottom of that ladder. He humbled me one day when he said the minute he sees preaching from a stage as being any more important or worthwhile than mopping these floors, he would have lost all perspective in life.

Why do companies like Google work so well when it comes to employee satisfaction? In my opinion, it is not because they get free food or mid-day napping pods (although I'm sure that stuff doesn't hurt). No, I think it is because the employees, no matter where they are, feel a sense of purpose and belonging. The companies invest back into the people to meet their needs, to make people the goal of a thriving company, not money and power. Now they are one of the largest and wealthiest companies.

When the person mopping your floors is seen to have as much worth as the person running the company, you change the culture in the dynamics of humility. Companies built around humility are the strongest, not the weakest. On the opposite side, companies built upon power are the driving forces of separation, isolation, depression and anxiety. I don't need to quote scientific research articles because I've sat with dozens of those folks who made it in that world. People who attained millions of dollars in wealth and power yet felt miserable and powerless within their own lives. Sadly, the societal drive and emphasis on wealth and power keeps them, as well as the rest of us, in a perpetual cycle of despair. How are we any different than a hamster on a wheel chasing after a carrot?

When people say they long for wealth and power, I can only chuckle at the amount of wealthy and powerful people who wish they could spend time with their kids or just go for a walk and find joy in their life again. We have it all backwards constantly looking at everyone else thinking we want what they have and THEN we will be happy. Our opportunity is not to say that I am better than you, our opportunity is to acknowledge that we all have value and worth and the success of the company is dependent upon us all. If you are an employee, invest in the livelihood of your co-workers. If you are lucky enough to have control of money in the company, then invest back into your employees, not a bigger house or nicer car.

When you build a company that is thriving based on interconnectedness and community, you build a company that integrates joy into its foundation. When a company has joy built into its foundation, it is not only going to be able to weather the storms better, it will be able to thrive in the storms. Many companies went under when the economy crashed in 2008. But some companies collectively worked together, as a whole, to make the sacrifices together to survive the turbulent times. Instead of everyone losing their jobs, everyone worked fewer hours, took pay cuts and shared hours with those struggling more than others.

If you build a company worth working for, employee satisfaction is higher, employee engagement is higher and the overall health of the company is higher. Would it be such a terrible thing to be a part of a company where people are excited to come to work most days? Where perhaps there was a bit less stress and chaos and more support and resources to survive difficult situations collectively or problem-solve more efficiently?

We need to get off our pedestals and high horses and breathe. Like having healthy relationships, we also need to invest into each other. I'm not asking anyone to take a bullet, I'm asking for safe environments to ask for help and to feel valued. You don't have to be Google in order to care about your employees.

Step 6 in trickle-out collaboration: bring the opposites together. Whoever you think is the most opposite person in your company, get lunch with them one time a week for a year. Make a new friend, learn about your commonalities, your differences, your struggles and accomplishments. If you are the highest paid person, meet with the lowest paid person. If you can't stand those people in "that" department, there is your clue. Don't hide in a private meeting room, meet in the cafeteria. Better yet, bring them a lunch you made from home. If you want to be at a company worth working for, show valuation in anyone and everyone. That is how you weather the storms and struggles, together.

CHAPTER 7 NOTES AND REFLECTIONS

How do you feel like your company supports and values your opinions? If not, how could that change? Do you feel like you and your co-workers would fight for each other's jobs or collectively take a pay-cut to move the company forward? If not, how could you move towards that? Does the relationship between the CEO and the janitor feel a million miles apart or in the office next door?

_____

_____

_____

_____

_____

_____

_____

_____

_____

_____

_____

_____

_____

_____

8

BEFRIENDING THE DARKNESS,

embrace imperfection

We are terrified of being perceived as anything short of perfect. Even if someone calls out a minor flaw in us, we tend to do one of several things; make an excuse for why the flaw occurred (making it not our fault), prove the person is wrong in their assumptions, or turn the tide back on the person making note of a significantly larger flaw in them.

Whether it is true or not, engage it. I can honestly promise you, without a shadow of a doubt, that you are, indeed, not perfect.

But unfortunately, as much as we joke about this, we actually tend to live our lives as though we are. It is toxic, it destroys relationships, it consumes our mental energies, it makes people act arrogant and disrespectful and it makes people avoid us at all costs. We have all been the jerk, we have all witnessed people acting like jerks. Meanwhile, we miss the opportunity for growth. There is an endless opportunity to learn from the less-than-perfect aspects of ourselves. It's time we stop running from it and embrace our imperfections; embrace our darkness.

This is not an opportunity to double down, and say, "It is what it is". This is an opportunity to engage, learn and evoke discernable change. Start with very plain honesty. You are going to make mistakes and let your employees and co-workers know that. Ask for feedback, ask for honesty and GIVE transparency. You want to have a strong company; make it based on vulnerability and empathy because no one can take that away from you. It's amazing how these simple concepts change the tone of an entire conversation. Don't fool yourself though, your pride and ego are strong and this will be harder than you might think.

We've all been a bully and we've all been bullied. How do you defeat a bully? You love them. You can fight them, sure, but now you are the bully. It's a vicious cycle that seems stuck on repeat. Some of the best advice I've ever received on bullying is when someone comes up and attempts to bully you, own it, and all of their power is taken away. "You're right, I have made that mistake before, do you have any suggestions for me?" "Yeah, this outfit doesn't match; it looks kind of silly, doesn't it?"

Bullying is all too prevalent in the work place. Give a person a bit of power and tie that into a bad day and they are likely to abuse it. We attack others when we are hurting so that way we don't feel small in our isolation and loneliness. This doesn't have to be the only way. When we embrace our imperfections, we take the strength of those who attack us away and we give others the opportunity to embrace their own imperfections by setting precedent.

Owning it, however, isn't enough. If I told you that you talk in a really demeaning way to my coworkers and I and in turn, you acknowledge that sometimes you can surely be a bit crude... great! But if you don't actually take time to listen to when, how, where, and attempt to get to the root of "why" you are being crude in the first place, nothing will change.

After acknowledgement, listen to the feedback. Don't respond, don't fight back, don't defend it, no matter how much it churns inside you or how badly you want to prove that person wrong. Take it home and sit with it. Write about it, talk to a friend about it, meditate on it, develop clarifying questions. It takes time to process our imperfections, it is extremely rare that you understand everything in a light bulb moment and even more rare that we ever make quick changes to resolve the issues at hand.

Engaging our shortfalls never comes easy. Instead of seeing an opportunity for personal growth and empowerment, we tend to see red and get our troops ready to go to battle. Why? Why is it so hard to accept that we have flaws? Why do we respond to someone who points out a flaw in us with pointing out three flaws in them?

We are taught that in order to be "enough" we must be perfect. Anything short of that means you are doing something wrong and are failing in life. That is never the case, yet our subconscious mind tells us otherwise. Perhaps you are coming from an insecurity of having control or power or the need to be right. We don't like to be wrong, especially if it means someone else is right. It is more likely that we will fight tooth and nail to keep our pride and egos intact no matter the cost. Who loses in that situation?

You do.

I grew up in an environment where you did not have to win an argument by being "right," you simply had to prove the other person was wrong. The desire to be right in our culture keeps the ceaseless cycles of frustrations and arguments going without any reason to communicate or compromise properly. When you fight back, when you belittle another, when you succumb to your anger and negative emotions, you allow the other person to remain in charge of your joy. You are the inevitable loser in the situation, even if it appears that you "won" at the end of the day.

In embracing our pitfalls, we have the opportunity to learn and grow. It is then that we can embrace a new opportunity to become better leaders, better co-workers and better friends. It is then that we can set the tone for others to compromise and communicate with us and we can all grow collectively as a whole, together.

If you don't believe me, look at how the polarization of our entire country is going with the inability of both sides to communicate and compromise with each other. This fighting will end with either significant change in the direction to come together, or the entire thing will collapse on itself. You don't have to go far into any history book to see which options we tend to choose. But don't worry, when everything is in tatters and all that remains are our prides and egos, we will still get to claim we were "right."

No, we all long for a better world than that. A world where everyone's voice can be heard because the collective company is a strong company. A strong company is a successful company. A successful company is a company that is making headway and change in the world. That is how we thrive, that is how we adapt, that is how long-term visions prevail.

It is time we befriend our own imperfections and stop pointing the finger elsewhere. If you want to take this deeper, I write about the concept of "I'm not as bad as that person" syndrome in *Running From Fear*. It takes personal work and only you can start that process. So make it tangible, take steps to befriend your darkness. Don't stay static. This is your golden opportunity to become a better person and that is a gift, a wonderful, free gift. Embrace it, learn from it.

Step 7 of trickle-out collaboration: own your imperfections. Make a list of your own imperfections. Can't think of any? Ask people close to you, they will have some. Reflect on them and how you can improve. Spend more time focusing on what you could do to make things better and less time worrying about what everyone else is doing wrong. This is your journey. Besides, if you become a truer, more whole you, others will follow.

CHAPTER 8 NOTES AND REFLECTIONS

What avenues do you create for co-workers and employees to share constructive criticism? Do you sit and listen carefully or do you fight back? What avenues do you create to embrace and learn from your own imperfections?

_____

_____

_____

_____

_____

_____

_____

_____

_____

_____

_____

_____

_____

_____

_____

PART 3

ACT

Actually do what you intend to do

"When the whole world is silent, even
one voice becomes powerful"
–Malala Yousafzai

9

PASSION,

you are unstoppable with it

The Tech Center at General Motors was once one of the largest employee campuses in the world. It is still impressive given all the changes in the industry where it entertains upwards of 20,000 employees and visitors on any given day. I'll never forget the first time I visited the campus. Never have I received as many looks as I did walking in through those front doors wearing jeans, a t-shirt and a baseball cap with a backpack strung over my shoulders.

People looked at me as though I was lost on my way to school touting their perfectly pressed suits and blouses eager for the opportunity to impress. In fact, in several years of visits, I never saw a single person wearing a baseball cap. It wasn't an intent to be disrespectful to the culture of the campus, it was an intent to be honest to who I was and am. I was the best at what I did, not because I held a PhD and 30 years of experience, but because I had deep passion for what I was doing.

Building a zero-waste project for a company with several hundred employees is complicated. Building a zero-waste project for over ten thousand employees is a real challenge.

It also had to encapsulate thousands of people who would uniquely visit the campus every day who would not receive any training or notifications. I had to be good, I had to be efficient, and I had to know my stuff. That's why I wasn't afraid to get dirty and sort through trashcans and jump into dumpsters. I would never do that if I were wearing a suit trying to impress everyone else.

When you engage work from an act of passion, you aren't concerned with impressing anybody. However, it tends to naturally happen because I was hungry for challenges; to continuously learn and improve. I was hungry to make things better. I didn't need anyone's approval for that.

But that's not what I experienced in the business world. I rarely met people who held that level of passion. What did I actually find? People looking for ways to make money, people looking at ways to gain more power, and people looking to make a better image for themselves. Playing the relentless politics was exhausting. I didn't care and I was tired of trying to blow smoke up the right person's back end in order to keep the hierarchal checks in balance.

I watched entire programs collapse over it, I watched projects take years when they could have taken weeks, I saw companies lose savings of thousands of dollars because one person was getting a kickback check. I watched things vanish because someone made a call without getting approval from another higher up, only to find out it was somebody's golfing buddy that keeps the contracts in place. I had people try and buy me out, give me money on the side to screw over friends and colleagues, even try and take out my own business partners.

The larger I grew, the more it happened. It was disgusting. It was pitiful. It was shameful. I grew tired of it. I didn't care about trying to make more profit, I wasn't about to go golfing or drink scotch to play "the game," and I certainly wasn't going to write a check to someone to "make things go smooth." Don't tell me it is what you have to do in order to get things done. No, doing the right thing is what you need to do in order to get things done. It is that simple. The rest comes out the back side of a bull.

Are you passionate about creating better welfare for your company and colleagues or are you passionate about creating better welfare for your bank account? I can promise you one leads to more joy and connection and another leads to more division, isolation, and long-term loss for everyone involved. I saw it in all the people I engaged with. Why do I say it with such confidence? It wasn't just watching everyone else. My ultimate desire for more growth and resources to save the world was the same desire that destroyed my passion for the work I was trying to do. I lost sight of the greater resources and impact of those around me when it became "the Thad show" and I was the one running it.

When we are all in it together, on the same team, that is what makes a group unstoppable. But we all have passions in this life, things we are good at and enjoy. Like we previously discussed, we cannot all hold our dream jobs in the perfect scenario, but it doesn't mean your passions should be ignored when they can bring so much benefit to the workplace.

It doesn't have to be colossal. Perhaps Jennifer is passionate about yoga; why not let her teach a class for the employees once a week? Steve loves healthy cooking; can you encourage him to put together a healthy-living diet plan? Sue is a painter; why do we tend to have such incredibly ugly offices with bland eggshell white walls or art that was bought at Bed Bath and Beyond? Let her spruce it up and paint a new mural each year where the team votes on what the theme is. As children, we are expressive and expansive. Kids bring light to our eyes with their imagination and creativity. As we grow older, that creativity is slowly killed to tame our spirits. We are not meant to be tamed, we are meant to be filled with boundless joy. Release some of the fruitless restraints and let people bring life back into the workplace in meaningful, creative ways.

When you are filled with life, you will only bring more life into your workplace, which will only trickle out into the lives of those around you. Why did you take this job or start this company in the first place? Was it just for money? I'm not buying it because that endeavor leaves you frustrated and depressed quickly in a never-ending pursuit of a temptation that cannot be fulfilled. No, I think you did this to make a change, to start new, to make an impact, to make a difference, to improve your life. Where is that passion and desire that led you to take the job or start that company in the first place? Because we all long to be inspired, we all long for something more.

Step 8 of trickle-out collaboration: cultivate your passions. There is nothing better than getting lost in a conversation where someone is riding the emotional high of his or her great passions. Even if their passion is not remotely one of mine. Stop right now and recall the last time you did that thing that you love. Not that thing you enjoy, that thing that makes you come alive. Were you doing that thing last week or are you like me where it has been months to years? Life is too short. We need you and we need that energy. Find a way to share that pure joy back with us. Remind us all just how good life can be.

CHAPTER 9 NOTES AND REFLECTIONS

What is it that you really want to do? Can you in some small way bring that into your company? How do you as an employer offer opportunities for your employees to follow their passions? How do, you as a co-worker, respect and support the passions of those around you?

10

TRANSPARENCY,

it is not a one time action, it is a defining character

W e often hide certain details that might portray a different story than the one we want to share, then go to great lengths to make sure the truth is never revealed. It is incredibly stressful and it is fatal to the soul of the company. I once worked with a company that owed me and my colleagues tens of thousands of dollars. We were actively buying them time and doing everything we could to support them while the weeks of waiting for payment turned into months. Turns out we weren't able to receive payment because that company was busy purchasing other companies in part due to the money owed to us. Let's just be politically correct and say it put a strain on year's worth of relationship building.

I've seen what happens when leaders crack down on employees watching their expenditures and inspecting every receipt to nitpick over a few dollars while personally taking home hundreds of thousands. Companies that claim little profits when it is sheltered elsewhere to make sure there is less profit to share with the employees. In fact, I have never known a company to share the true cost of a product they purchased, always sneaking in some additional numbers before telling a wise tale.

Lies, white lies, variations of the truth, proprietary information, whatever fable is used to justify the relentless attempts to conceal is futile. Secrets ultimately destroy the integrity of a company. At the very least, they create divisions and barriers that dismantle the relationships of employees within. This is the one aspect of this work that should begin in the hands of the leaders. The power for leadership to be vulnerable sets the tone that all things are possible.

I'm not talking about revealing Bush's Baked Beans recipe here or the secret mathematical formula for a product you don't even have a patent on. But some of the best companies are those that are open and honest. When I worked for World Centric, the leadership team went through a process of TEAL training in an attempt to create a more transparent environment and create ownership in the staff. All cards were on the table including, but not limited to; profit and loss statements, company directions and values, new company divisions, and even community impact. Employees were encouraged to take ownership in specific projects to grow and add new ideas.

The more transparent a company is, the more the company is able to celebrate the effort and good times collectively and feel like all persons are a part of the success. But it also enables the opportunity for members to strategize when things aren't going so well, to be a part of the solution. I've watched entire companies shut down behind closed doors without attempting to even consult or allow employees to partake in the change or help save the company.

The only reason to hide these details would be based on a lack of trust in pursuit of control or shame and guilt over what others may think. But if the goal is a company of strength, then trust must be established in order to set the tone. And if there is fear over what others may think about, for example, your salary, then perhaps that should be a reflection of what the end goals of the company are for. Too often I've seen CEOs take home six and seven figure incomes while paying janitorial staff minimum wage. Take time to consider the message that sends to someone about their worth in trying to make a living or support a family in doing a job you are likely not willing to do.

"There is a moral imperative to lead and do the right thing for those you are leading"

Dan Price, CEO of Gravity, said this when he took a 90% pay-cut from his one-million-dollar salary down to $70,000 to share it with his 120 employees who now all receive a minimum of $70,000 in salary. The result three years later? The revenues continue to grow, Gravity holds 40% more employees, and employee satisfaction has never been higher.

Transparency and vulnerability from the leader built an already successful company, like Gravity, into an even greater company, all while doing the best thing for the employees and the community. It isn't rocket science, no matter how much we try and make it. Treat your employees well and the company will do better. Be open and honest and the company will do better. If there are kinks, they will be naturally worked out collectively.

One more note on transparency. This isn't all about dollars and sense (pun intended). This is also about vulnerability on a personal level. I'm not suggesting one divulges every personal detail to the world or work place. But there is strength in admitting that things may be hard. We often separate ourselves in our pursuit to present our lives as perfect. Perfect marriage, perfect kids, perfect vacations, perfect friends, perfect pets. But no one's life is ever perfect. When we are able to step out of our comfort zone and admit that we don't have it all together, it reminds others that we are indeed human.

Take a chance and see if you aren't surprised to see that you have more in common with that person you avoid at all costs at the office. Who knows, perhaps you may have a real conversation that doesn't involve sports or the weather. Maybe, you might even share commonalities that lead to new growth and learning in your own life.

Step 9 in trickle-out collaboration: transparency. Admit that you might not be perfect. Admit that you make mistakes. Admit that you could be wrong. Admit that things can be difficult. Admit that you might not know. Find strength in transparency and vulnerability. Remember, it isn't just business because businesses are run by humans and like it or not, we are all in this together. So share. Information, wealth, resources, power...share it. It will only make the community stronger.

CHAPTER 10 NOTES AND REFLECTIONS

How would your employer/employees say that the company is transparent? Do you feel like your opinions matter or are considered in the company? How would you want to make more impact or would you want your employees to make more impact/have more ownership in the company? Do you offer the opportunity? Do you share your triumphs as well as some of your struggles? Do you create safe platforms for vulnerability without judgment?

_____

_____

_____

_____

_____

_____

_____

_____

_____

_____

_____

_____

_____

_____

_____

11

WHAT IS YOUR SOCIAL PROGRAM?

As a verb, not a once a year noun.

Give back and give back freely.

You did not make it this far on your own. No matter how hard you tried, no matter how many handouts you didn't receive, no matter how much you had to pull yourself up by your own bootstraps, you did not do it alone. In the very simplest of arguments, two people had to come together for your existence. No matter how good or bad your childhood was, you did not enter this world alone. Millions, literally millions, of moments had to take place in order to get you to this exact moment you are in today while reading this. Millions had to happen in order for me to be able to share these pages with you.

We cannot do this on our own. There is strength in admitting our interdependence, not weakness. We need one another to survive and that should be our first act of humility; acknowledge you cannot do it alone. When you can begin to accept this, we can begin to remember all the ways in which others have helped us along the way, or given us a chance, or perhaps given us a break or a bit of forgiveness when we didn't think we deserved it. There was nothing better than a teacher who gave us an extra day to do our homework or a boss who let us off the hook the first time we were late. But it comes in the bigger items. Like when people take chances on us. To start a new job or start a new friendship, we are putting trust in a person.

We do not just receive in financial means. We receive in relational means, in means of opportunity, in means of fate or chance, we receive regardless of how we may or may not define our worth. We have moments we feel on top of the mountain and we have moments when we feel like we are drowning in a flood. The key to remember is the golden rule – what would you want if it were you at the bottom of the hill? Would you want someone to help you or give you an opportunity? Of course, you cannot get anywhere in this life without it.

So even if you aren't on top of the mountain, give what you can and give freely. There is always someone in need, someone who could use a helping hand. A friend who's struggling to pay bills, an elderly person who feels abandoned and forgotten about in a retirement home, an eager person waiting for someone to give them a chance at more, a person looking for a meal, or a person looking for someone to listen. You know why this is so crucial? Because when we give unconditionally to others, without expectations or promises of anything in return, we will find ourselves surrounded by those who care when the phone call comes from the doctor, or our bank account is lower than expected, or when we don't want to go to the funeral alone.

"The best way to find yourself is to lose yourself in the service of others"

It is my favorite quote by Gandhi and is one of the first things I see when I wake up each morning. I want to take a moment here as we being to wrap up this book to make one very blunt statement. Your wealth, the bigger house, the larger savings account, the stuff you are accumulating, it is all worthless and will bring you no real joy in the end. Breathe, you are either frustrated with me or you know it to be true, but either way, just breathe.

Our society tells us that our worth is dependent upon our wealth and what we have accomplished in this life. To quote Dr. Brené Brown, "We are the most in-debt, obese, addicted and medicated adult cohort in U.S. history." Her work speaks volumes to this as she helped inspire me to write *Running From Fear*. There was a gift in losing all of my wealth and there were even more gifts in working with terminally ill patients. When I worked on the oncology floor at the hospital as a nurse's aide, I was able to sit with dozens of patients who shared some of their final wisdoms with me. People who were financially worth millions and people who were financially worth nothing. Whether the patient was in their 20s, 40s, 60s or 80s, there was a familiar story; the money, the jobs, the to-do lists, the accumulated stuff, the anger, the fights, the pride and the egos, it was all meaningless at the end of the day. What mattered most were the relationships left standing at the bedside.

Donating $20 to that organization during the holidays or volunteering once a year will not suffice. Giving is a verb, not a noun. Like exercise, we must continually do it in order to remain healthy and strong.

We all long for a purpose at the end of the day and that purpose is meaningless if it is not greater than ourselves. Instead of burning bridges or toppling others for the sake of business, growth and profits, invest in each other. Invest in your communities. A tree gives us the oxygen we need to breathe as a part of its life cycle, it gives freely to us without question, without asking what we will do with the precious breath we've been provided, without wondering whether we will use that breath for good or use that breath to cut the forest down. The trees will continue to give regardless.

We must become like trees in our community taking in the resources we have to survive in this life and transforming them into something better to serve those around us, freely and without conditions or expectations. There are countless organizations, projects, people, and environmental issues that need your help. You've been given a gift in this circle of life so don't let the circle end with you.

Step 10 is our final step in trickle-out collaboration:

GIVE BACK FREELY.

CHAPTER 11 NOTES AND REFLECTIONS

What is your social mission personally and as a business? What ways do you give your time, energy or resources back into the community and the world? What brings you life? Are you able to share that life with others? What projects can you collectively do with your co-workers and employees?

_____

_____

_____

_____

_____

_____

_____

_____

_____

_____

_____

_____

_____

12

ENOUGH WITH THE FLUFFY, WHERE'S THE REAL WORLD?

Short, blunt next steps

B y now, someone has inevitably said, "this all sounds nice in theory, but this is the real world and things need to get done." Exactly, this is the real world, this is your world, so make it a good one. Make it better, improve it. Don't settle for mediocrity of "we got it done." Do something. Be bold. Make a change. It starts with you. Will everyone respond the way you think they ought to? No. But that doesn't mean you should sacrifice the content of your character to match it. Do you want your voice and your opinion and your objectives to be heard? Then you need to do one very specific thing.

Listen.

Do you have time to listen to everyone's perspective on every topic? No, but there needs to be valid outlets for all employees to embrace and share their creativity and insights. That is how we innovate and become the next driving force in our community. I don't mean listen while doing emails or responding to that text. Listen. Ask questions, let go of what you are planning to say next and listen. Let go of the notion of being right, let go of the notion of waiting for a break to interject. When your time comes, don't take ten minutes for what could be said in three. Be respectful of everyone's time so they are more likely to listen to you.

"Most people do not listen with the intent to understand; they listen with the intent to reply." – Stephen R. Covey

------

To be heard is to be known.

If you really have something to say, first you need to listen to others and hear what they are saying. I promise you that if you sit and give your full attention to someone, they will be more likely to listen to you. When both parties can be heard and known, there is a great opportunity for perspective.

- Perspective leads to compromise.

- Compromise leads to action.

- Unified actions lead to changes.

- Changes lead to growth and success; however you define it.

Live true to it.

Whatever your values are, live true to them. If you want people to be kind and compassionate, then be kind and compassionate to others. If you want to be a jerk, then be a jerk to others and they will likely be a jerk back to you. Define your values and live true to them. Acknowledge first and foremost that other people exist, they may not share your same values, and that is okay. But if your business is growing, it likely means someone else's business is shrinking.

There is not an infinite amount of growth on a planet filled with finite resources. Companies live and die, people are hired and fired, and when you land that new account, acknowledge the pain that someone else lost theirs. When you land that new job, acknowledge you likely took someone else's. And when you leave, acknowledge that someone has to fill the gap.

So when you define the values collectively or individually, don't put them on a plaque in your waiting room; no one takes that seriously anyways. If you are living true to your values, you don't need to put them on a plaque because everyone can already see them being carried out. But someone needs to take the first step. If you are the leader, that means the ball is in your court; don't wait for your employees to do it for you and show them how it is done. If you are an employee, that means the ball is in your court too, don't wait for your boss to ask you do it; set the precedent for how it should be done.

Patience

Not everything is going to go your way all the time, not even most of the time. Change takes time. It sucks, it is incredibly frustrating, and we always know exactly how things should go if everyone would just do x, y and z. But we don't actually have any guarantees. You do not know for 100% certainty that if you did or changed that thing it would have a different outcome just like you don't know with 100% certainty that if you do or change this thing you will have a specific outcome in the future.

If you think you have that much control, sit with someone who just survived an earthquake and whose business is in a pile of rubble. Sit with the mother of three who found out she has months left to live. Sit with a father who lost his daughter in a car accident when she just went out to get ice cream.

––––––––––––

Grace

It is not your job to control everything so breathe. But that is not an excuse to not do your best. You can start a new company and fail. You can save a co-worker's job and they may still dislike you. Lots of things can go wrong with the best of intentions. But if you are doing your best, then you never have to wonder "what if _____." With the best of plans, things will <u>not</u> go according to plan. That is okay. People will mess things up, you will mess things up, and some things will just happen.

This is not a journey without flaws and this is not a journey to become flawless. This is a journey to try and make tangible changes, to say that we can go beyond the status quo for our company and for each other. Life is short, we all know that, but we hardly ever live that way. Grace extends the deepest roots of change to all aspects of our lives. If the only thing we change is offering more grace to ourselves and those around us, the company, workplace and community will already be better off than it was before.

We are all waiting for someone to take the first step – be bold, why shouldn't that person be you?

_____

May you find grace and resilience on your journey. You are taking a step just in reading this and I am grateful for it. And thank you for all the gifts you share with the world, even the ones you don't know you have.

THE 10 LISTED STEPS TO TRICKLE-OUT COLLABORATION

(in case you need to borrow for a PowerPoint slide):

1. Admit your fears
2. Redefine enough
3. Self-care
4. Inward reflections
5. Define your image
6. Bring the opposites together
7. Own your imperfections
8. Cultivate your passions
9. Transparency
10. Give back freely

For more information, seminars, speaking engagements, podcasts, other books and upcoming events, visit:

www.ThadCummings.com
or contact at: info@ThadCummings.com

WANT TO TAKE IT A STEP FUTHER? CHECK OUT THIS OTHER TITLE BY THAD CUMMINGS

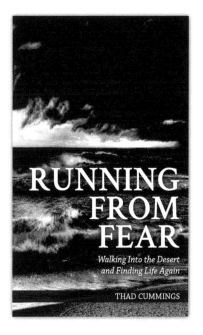

There is no shortage of good books, friends, support groups, therapies, religious teachings, advice and knowledge on how to live a life full of abundance, joy and love. Yet, in so many lives, it barely exists. Fear is the roadblock that keeps us from engaging a life we all desire, but cannot seem to get to because it is always somewhere over there, just out of reach. From our jobs to our relationships, from our past pain to our current despair, to all the negativity that clouds our communities, fear affects everyone, universally. This is a conversation with stories about how we can engage the fears we all face so that they are no longer controlling our lives. This is about turning knowledge into practical wisdom.